D0844245

LOVE IN THE LAST DAYS

LOVE IN THE LAST DAYS
AFTER TRISTAN AND ISEULT

D. Nurkse

ALFRED A. KNOPF
New York
2017

THIS IS A BORZOI BOOK
PUBLISHED BY ALFRED A. KNOPF

Copyright © 2017 by D. Nurkse

All rights reserved. Published in the United States by Alfred A. Knopf,
a division of Penguin Random House LLC, New York, and distributed in Canada
by Random House of Canada, a division of Penguin Random House Canada Limited, Toronto.

www.aaknopf.com

Knopf, Borzoi Books, and the colophon are registered
trademarks of Penguin Random House LLC.

Library of Congress Cataloging-in-Publication Data
Names: Nurkse, D., 1949– author
Title: Love in the last days : after Tristan and Iseult / by D. Nurkse.
Description: First edition. | New York : Alfred A. Knopf, 2017.
Identifiers: LCCN 2016058422 (print) | LCCN 2017006210 (ebook) |
ISBN 9780451494801 (hardback : alk. paper) | ISBN 9780451494818 (ebook)
Subjects: | BISAC: POETRY / American / General.
Classification: LCC PS3564.U76 A6 2017 (print) | LCC PS3564.U76 (ebook) | DDC 811/.54—dc23
LC record available at https://lccn.loc.gov/2016058422

*Jacket image by Johann Friedrich Hennings. Interfoto/A. Koch/Mary Evans
Jacket design by Kelly Blair*

Manufactured in the United States of America

First Edition

For Beth, with love

The story of the lovers Tristan and Iseult reverberates throughout the Middle Ages.

Set in Ireland, England, and Brittany—or their mythic counterparts—the legend keeps resurfacing, each time with a new twist: a fireside Celtic epic about a bold soldier, a French troubadour song, a self-aware courtly romance.

With gratitude and deep respect for the original texts of Gottfried von Strassburg, Thomas of Britain, and Béroul, and the scholarship of Joseph Bédier, this is my own version. It takes place in an imaginary past known as The Last Days.

Contents

Avalon

The King's Prison

LOVE IN THE LAST DAYS

Prelude

1

My father was a harper. So was his.
I memorized the notes to forget them.
On the ball of each finger, mark of a string:
the Old One, the Servant, Master of Melody.

But this story is strange to me
like wine tasted in a lover's mouth.

2

Tristan won Iseult by killing a snake
and took her to be his King's bride.
Or: for the sake of ruling Logres
and freeing Ireland, she sailed with him.

In a few measures she'll touch his wrist.

3
Let the words turn to music.

The modes advance of their own accord:
Ionian to Lydian, Locrian to Phrygian,
Aeolian to Dorian, a dominant cadence,
and back to tonic: Tristan will fetch her
to wed King Mark, then rescue her

to the forest, they'll know each other,
separate, grow old in bitter marriages,
and die of plague or a misunderstanding.

Theme, melody, recapitulation, coda.

———

This world is cruel, even to itself.
The white lilies prey on the blue.
Next comes Avalon, Land of the Living,
where the eye may keep what it sees.

4
Iseult steps to the rail, staring back at Ireland.

She doesn't fear death, only exile
and the wildness of the minor chords.

Tristan clears his throat.

The Sea

The Philtre

Tristan

Ireland turned to smoke in the West.

The beacons of Ui Cumain lined up and glinted
with the scary weakness of fire in sunlight.

We were becalmed. No doubt Echeneis,
the delay-fish, had latched on to our keel
with lantern jaws, dragging us backwards.

Under an awning rigged on the stern deck
I prepared to serenade Iseult. She rolled her eyes.

My larynx hardened in her gray stare.
My vocal cords tangled. I couldn't find *la,*
hidden in the past or future. I sang.

It seemed a distant instrument was accompanying me,
mocking at first, then creepy-tender.
When I stopped it fell silent. Perhaps
a scrim of spray had sharped my pitch.

I hated her for paying rapt attention to each false note
while the song of lovers at Avalon bored her.

That breakdown in technique—lapsed notulii
and spastic moduli—baffled me
like a fart in the presence of a Queen.
She giggled, saying, *You sing like a girl*.

I offered to teach her a few scales.
She hummed the grace notes.

———————

I challenged her at chess, determined
to let her win, but she won anyway.

To annoy her, I moved like lead,
waved the rook in midair, touched pawns
and my dog's nose, hummed to myself.

But she countered without thought,
eyes on the horizon. She castled long.

It struck me we were both a little leery
of the queen's power, the king's strange weakness,
bishops glaring down incompatible diagonals.

Once the ship pitched and a black pawn
slid all the way down the knight's file
and she caught it in the palm of her hand.
You are a Queen too now, she said.

When we looked over the bulwark
we saw each other clearly, staring back
from deep water, young and trembling.

That blue-green gaze held a determination
foreign to our lives. In reflection, we joined hands
gravely and without pressure. Yet at the rail
she kept a table-width between us.

She had the right. I killed the Irish monster
and won her to marry a king she never saw.
It made sense to me but not to her. Checkmate.

I put the pieces back in their gilt box.
I could not help running a finger
over their green baize pads.

I praised the court's elegance,
the chamber with its own hardwood fire,
the bed veiled for sleepless dreams.

She scoffed. *Better the cold quiet*
of my father's cottage in Morne
than fucking a toothless majesty.

I tried to reassure her. At Logres
we also had chipped chamber pots,
arras mildewing in dank corridors.

She waved off my comfort like a gnat.

I told her the status of my wound,
how it hurt always, like another soul,
and reminded her how I acquired it,
freeing her people from the rule of fangs.

She breathed lightly through pursed lips.

I expounded obliquely
on the art of dragon hunting,
the doctrines of Piraeus and Salmagor.

She scratched for lice
with an infuriating involuntary delicacy.

The crew hoisted rampart sails.
But the calm deepened. The prow
inched forward like a presentiment.
Two green bubbles trailed in our wake and popped.

We lay stranded on that breathless mirror
between her father's scrub oak

---

that she would never see again
and Logres, falsified in the Aeolian mode.

She stared ahead with narrow eyes.

I reasoned: at best you could have married a marguillier
and grown old in a tamped-clod hall,
flattered by a harp with catgut strings.

She answered: *Better a bed of forest twigs.*
The Logrian king adores me for a lock of hair
when I don't know who I am.

Her high cheekbones made me slightly seasick.
I concentrated on her faults, as Ovid advises.
A mole on her cheek. But that was what fascinated me.

I sent for venison and brushed away the maggots
but she made a face. Her servant Brangien brought wine.
Iseult wiped the rim with her wimple
and sipped and gagged.

That liquor tasted of honey and bile.

A voice yelled: *Wind.* The deck bucked.
The chalice slipped and shattered. My dog
licked the shards and moaned at the air between us.

The Hold

Tristan

She stared as I struggled with her kirtle,
vissoir and mandemain. Then we were naked.
Except for her eyes.

I was scared. I'd been naked in combat,
never in love. It seemed a bad omen.
Her cheek was too sheer. The keel shook
below us. We were gathering speed.

We took turns on top
as on a calm and dubious ocean
and found no fathom line, no strait home.

We lay under each other and found no shelter.

We rolled together, stunned
to have found an act so hard and easy,
or rested watching our transport
in detachment. We both knew how it ends.

Joy leads to sadness, sadness to bitter joy.

At twilight I gagged and ducked out
and shucked back apologizing.
Terror of her beauty made me queasy,
not the swerving hold.

I begged a clove. She had tinctures.
She gave me cardamom. But it tasted of her.
Her mossy armpits, like my nurse's long ago,
smelled faintly sour, of windfall apples.

A torch poked in and retreated.
She shielded me with her matted hair.

In that sudden flare, I remembered
we were damned in two worlds.

She bit me and giggled and made a snake noise.
She ran her little finger over my wound,
three puncture marks at my hip.

She whispered my name, but backwards,
since we were not made for each other,
but to be the other's obstacle,
cherished and loathed like the self.

A stain glittered between us, a map
of a country in which we could not live—
any kingdom in this world.

A hoarse thrilled cry rose high above us—
a king's name or just the word: land?

Tantris, she said, and that's who I am.

Logres

The Defense   *Tristan*

While Iseult lay in the King's arms
I played chess against myself.
How powerfully I opened with the king's pawn,
two squares, how cunningly I countered
with the king's pawn, one square.
I strove to exploit my weakness,
the pawn that the king alone defends.
I took advantage of my premature attack—
the infantry was locked in phalanxes,
fianchettoed bishops stared at each other,
rooks piled on closed corridors—
when I heard her hoarse cry. Was it my name?
It could not have been. I would be dead.
I was in zugzwang, there was no move.
Each strategy predicted itself.
I had created a world the opposite of action
while Iseult moved as recklessly as God.
She made Brangien sleep with the King
and ordered her death, to silence the act.
Who was this Queen? The night wind?
Still I understood: she was protecting me.
If she wasn't a virgin on her wedding night
I would be summoned and interrogated.

The King's prison will change you more than death.

Why didn't she consult me? Or send news?
I refused to surrender and knocked the pieces
so the kings rolled in concentric circles,
tiny crosses pointing inwards—now to wait
for midnight, the hour of secret messages
written in my mouth by a lithe silent tongue.

The Servant

Brangien

I

All my life I pour, and one slip:
I gave the wrong wine to a clumsy knight.

Iseult sent me to service the King.
She coiffed herself as a scullery maid
and painted and undressed me
in white-lipped silence. When a candlewick
snuffed the dripping tapers, I entered
that darkness like the pupil of the eye,
sensed stale air, and found the massive oak bed.
I knew the King by his wine breath. He rolled on top.
I thought of home, my croft in Ireland.

I saw it from a distance, smoke from the peat hearth
like the string to a child's toy.
I pried the creaky door open and sat down
with my father and mother and broke black bread.
Far away the King labored in the heavy seas
of his one-person wedding.

I touched him a little in pity. I kissed him once
lightly on the earlobe. He came in a clamor
of groans and mumbles, then in a broken voice
began giving me the great gifts: gerfalcon, ocelot,
the palfrey Beau Joueur, the pear orchard.
A stain oozed between us. I touched my blood to his lips.
He licked his fingers, curled in a ball, and slept.
I dressed in darkness. The shift I put on was darkness.
I groped for the door. There was the Queen
waiting on tiptoe. She didn't thank me.

I felt the wind of her hands, avid for the headboard
as she entered the night of her marriage.

All my life I polish a mirror
that was too bright to start with.

2

Iseult ordered me to the forest to be killed.
Because I knew she cheated? I bedded her King?
Because my mistake bound her to Tristan—
good singer, reasonable swordsman, sentimental in bed?

She sent me with a shepherd to gather chanterelles.
He took me—so quickly—to the shadow of Morois
and watched as I fumbled with boletes
that broke too easily, like flesh.
He tested his knife and I begged him *no*.

I have power too: am I not the victim?

Gottfried of Strassburg says Christ
is like an old shirt
that takes any shape you choose.

When we emerged into twilight
the Queen was waiting, wringing her hands—
always waiting, that dark Queen!

She embraced me. Since she was royalty,
ordained by God, she had no power to repent,
but I felt her tears on my own cheek,
a little too salty—she had been making love—
and that night the shepherd disappeared.

3

All my life I sweep
and the rim of the pan
leaves an ever-finer line of dust.

———————

Assignations   *Tristan*

1
I trembled before each meeting, and trembled after.

Hidden outside her tower, I charmed Iseult with birdsong.
Thrush ecstatic but with a questioning hiccup,
obsessive wheedling finch, indifferent wren,
heartbroken nightingale, ironic cuckoo.

She never answered. Brangien fetched me at midnight.

2
I stepped into the Queen's gray eyes and crossed the horizon.
During the dry-mouth moment together, I spoke in platitudes
of Avalon, Island of Immortality, how our grief
will have no body to house it, and batter against those shores,
but those cliffs are granite and there are paths
only the goats know, and the fisher martens, and the newly dead.
I told her of Ysinvitrain, further north, the Glass Kingdom,
where all things are transparent, bread and the knife to cut it,
even the invisible wound, even a lover's mind, and the eye itself.
I realized I was babbling about death, like a child
who found a feather, and I forced myself to compliment her
on her hair knot, her obsidian clasp. She was so vivid
I could not look at her directly, even when I was on top of her.
It was like praising a fire. She stopped listening.
When I caught my breath—always during the meetings my breath
surged against me—she prodded me with questions:
Where could a boat land under those screes? Then the encounter
was over. We had slept together. Or not. I said good-bye
as you might take leave of night itself. In the third watch
I was almost happy to be me, just another sword, paid off

with a title, allowed to doze armed cap-à-pie in the royal chamber
among the alaunts' hot mouths, and dream of the King's bed.

3
Alone, I could almost see and touch her, when we made love
she was faes, the caul of the Absolute hid her naked body.

The Grail   *Tristan*

I

We subdued a village at the edge of Morois—
a toothless hag scraping a bloody sheepskin, a cripple planing
a board of knotty pine, a child plucking a crow, a few girls,
dizzy with hunger, stumbling in the fuller's ditch,
sweat sticking burlap dresses to spindleshanks.

How their dogs' eyes widened when we came riding out of the brush,
out of the play of light and shadow, with our crested plumes,
Toledo steel and argent-gules escutcheon.

We lined the men at spearpoint and asked: Have you seen the Grail?
And they asked: What Grail? We were at a loss there.
It was Iseult's obsession and our desire to be perfect for her,
to be good on the bloody earth, so that God would love us
and lift that long stalemate: death without end, or grace.

Allegedly it was a jar that held Christ's blood, now empty.
We cupped our hands, describing it, and the manants pointed vaguely.
Perhaps there, in Morois, where the fires burn all summer?
There, in the Fosse Commune, the fever bog? If they had not tried
to trick us—if a child hadn't mimicked our cupped hands—

we reared back on our destriers and left those mud-daubed cabins
wreathed in flames—lance to the banked coals,
thrust to the wattle—and rode on in silence
in the chill of evening with the smell of smoke
growing a little stronger at each trick of the wind
and every path we chose was one they had suggested.

2

That mighty adventure eluded us.

I could not you tell what it is: a cup, a dish, a trophy,
Joseph of Arimathea's chipped vessel: a mystery to give us
the power over ourselves that we have over others.

All we had to show the Queen was wounds: Borhold
his mangled thumb, Bors his sutured belly,
Palafox his missing eyelid.

My wound displayed no scab, no blemish.
No flailing axe made it, no pot of lit oil.
Yet it was me she chose. *Tristan, show me your wound.*

The King's Chamber   *Tristan*

A gazehound, dozing with eyes open,
stared at me with a profound knowing ignorance.
His nostrils flared, inhaling my lineage
and venal sin, without interrupting his dream.

I crept into the bedroom and lay among the dogs:
Castilian alaunts with ears trimmed to points,
who sleep in armor, dim-witted mastiffs, so imitative
they might nip a spurred horse, terriers
trembling to flush out imaginary enemies.

Each snored according to his breed.
Elkhounds snoozed on top of otterhounds.
Beagles hunted in obsessive unreal circles.
Greyhounds rippled with trance sprints. So dogs too
have a voice that tells them not to act in dreams.

My own mutt curled up at a distance, ashamed to know me.

The kennets and harriers twitched and writhed,
from their thick faint furious cries I deduced
a wounded rabbit, a feist in heat, an adored master,
as Apollonius says we surmise a world from the evidence
of our uncontrollable senses. Sometimes a sleeper drooled
on my cheek, or pinned my wrist with a paw,
or enclosed my ankle with a soft in-bite
exactly like the pang of my own dreams.

Once I drowsed and woke with a scabrous tongue
curling in my mouth. A bloodhound glanced at me

with lugubrious cloudy eyes, and when I started,
rolled to the wall with an absent moan.

So loudly they slept in a vortex of breath
on the straw bed, among bones gnawed to shards,
while snow tumbled like dice in a high slit window
and two guards slept upright, leaning on spears.

Out of that roar of panting and muffled cries
I heard Iseult's breath, a thread I followed
all the way back to childhood, to the first night
when my mother died birthing me in the birch forest.

Then I crawled onto that high oak bed
and snuggled between the monarchs. He murmured thickly,
darling, I answered in a thin voice, darling.

I turned to my Queen and in that darkness
we thought to enter the pupil of God's eye
before he created us, when he was surprised
the light he made to end his loneliness was good.

We loved each other as we are commanded to, politely,
efficiently, with the King's dreaming arm covering us,
until the cock crowed at false dawn
and a faint bell tolled matins.

I whispered good-bye and slithered over bunched pugs
who shivered with a milder, more inward twitch,
beginning to negotiate endings to their dreams,
commencing to know each other and trade soft nips.
Their eyes lit, but not yet with the light of the mind.

I passed like a thought between the spearheads
and vanished down the winding torchlit corridors.
I reached my chamber, bolted the door,
congratulated myself and stumbled

because I was walking in blood. That secret joy
had reopened my wound and a trail led back
from my cold bed to the King's embrace.

The trumpet sounded fortissimo *wake, wake*,
about to crack in the cold.

Escape

I don't remember how I passed the portcullis.
I slipped into the hedgerows to wait for a sign.
But nothing. Bells tolling nones, fornication, lauds,
betrayal, angelus, judgment, all ran together
as if time were a single moment.

I had made a tourniquet of a strip of arras.
Despite my tremor, the wound closed.

I had slipped in one night from knight to thief.
Not just adulterous but dishonored.
Not just a traitor, a coward.
I realized what it cost to love Iseult.

I thought *fol'amor* would be a lacerating fire.
It deadened me to white ash.
I thought to make a promise I could keep or break.
It sealed me out of my life.
I was damned. But I could reason backwards
and explain my flight.

If I was taken, truth would be tortured out of me.
Since I hid, the King might grant her innocence
and condemn me. The proofs were just my absence
and a line of bloody footprints.

So I stared from a halo of serrated elm leaves
at that castle intricate as a rich child's toy.

Banners and pinions billowed and sank.
Drawbridges rose and fell. Plumed hordes
poured out with tiny raised spears, then swarmed back.

My eye caressed a single high blank window.

How I hoped Iseult would denounce me.
If she claimed I forced her, I could return
and hang like a manant. But I knew her silence.
It's invincible. Even her words are silent.
Her very thoughts. I rubbed nettles on my face,
tore my clothes, pretended to be mad
and mumbled on the berms of a famine village
where serfs comment on the mishaps of the rich.

At nightfall I overheard news.

The Queen had been given to a leper.

The Leper

Ivain

I was asked politely to stand in my open grave
and recite: *Of my own free will I choose*
to wear this pointed cap,
this black jute hauberk
with a muslin placket fastened with twine.

Our Lord was a leper, but because of my sins
I promise never to caress a child,
never touch a well rope, never eat from a dish,
never marry, never enter a mill,
church, fair, market or narrow lane.

Yet I looked no different from them.
In all their pictures, there were pustules.
I had none. Still the children
drew me in dust and called me "pustule."
I had to refrain from answering.

The breeze was my master. I had to maneuver myself
downwind when spoken to.

They said I had been conceived in menopause,
in coitus frigidi or calidi,
unclean like a rabbit or camel.

I had a little bell to ring constantly. At first
my wrist ached. Later, in dreams, I missed that ringing.
It made me invisible. I walked between winds.

A farm girl came to me in secret
between river and creek, between dusk and twilight.

While we fucked I had to ring my bell
or they would wake from that trance they called my sickness.

I rang it with my foot and when I came
they thought it was a carillon
announcing another of the King's wars.

But when she was pregnant what could she do
but sleep with a serf, marry him,
spread her legs for the King?

So I grew old in the narrow precinct of that name—leper.
I wore an L of damask which slowly faded to dust.
I grew dull with the belled cat and blinkered nag.

It was rumored I would die, if not in a year
in a decade or an instant.

But desire burned me when I saw my love
grown fat and mild with a brood of children.

What had touched me? Not even a breath—a breeze.
Not even a word: a name.
How could I suffer when I had to constantly sing
De Profundis in a small aggrieved voice?
I had the same hunger you do,
and the stray dogs and sparrows—
the hunger to be touched, like a knife between my legs.

Then the criers told me
I was to be given the Queen.
The King was sulking
because she had known a vassal.
They brought her bound to my hut.
One of them stood outside
ringing my bell for me

while another cried: De Profundis.
The Queen slept on the inside of the pallet
with her hands as a pillow, trying not to touch the straw,
making herself small, her hair in her mouth against the stench

and I was at last allowed to blow out my candle
and lie in darkness, hers and mine.
We talked for a few hours—
I was a lazar, she was faes:
Iseult, like the sound of rain
that you might love for no reason.

When I woke there was the imprint of her cheek
hot beside me, and horsemen arriving and departing,
self-important in the weakness of dawn.

The guards gave me back the bell
and told me to resume suffering
but I had forgotten how.
I felt only that small intimate fire.
The L stood for the fifth letter of a dream.
They showed me, with whips and swords,
how they made each other suffer.

To appease them I rang my bell,
but softly, just for her, in that enchantment,
leprosy, and the pines writhed in the trance of wind.

Rescue *Tristan*

Iseult and the leper lay snoring on a pallet.
I didn't wake them. I sheathed my sword.
I carried my Queen to the waiting roan.
She came to with a soft cry. We galloped
towards the interior: at first a stain at horizon
then fallow earth, a thicket, at last the wild,
that you enter like the ocean or a dream.
You choose an entry no bigger than your body
(my horse's body, but I willed myself to think
our horse, since we'd become a household in solitude).
The supple catkins drew a net around us,
oak with fat pleats at each tufted twig.
We entered shadow. She was crying.
I asked why. Tears answered. I was angry.
I exposed my life to free her
and risked the taint of pox. I reproached her.
She replied with a strange bitterness

*I will come with you of my own free will
into the heart of winter.*

The Horse   *Beau Joueur*

So we galloped towards Morois.

Or rather, I galloped, Tristan spurred.
Ahead of us the forest lay and soon towered
—there is no path to enter, you enter
by choice after forced choice, until
it hurts like fate: duck, swerve and squeeze
between almost-clearing and almost-thicket
constrained by the rhythm of gaps between trunks,
zones of ignorance between those lordly names

PINE CEDAR OAK ROWAN YEW SYCAMORE BIRCH.

The play of light and shadow intensified
and we were inside, as if inside the mind,
where you can only be in one thought, infinitely far
from all other thoughts, and all thoughts are equal.

He thought of her, she thought of winter.
Or so I surmise. Her hand held the reins
with such subtlety I could have been ruled
by God's will or the night wind.

So we entered Morois. Had it been Brocéliande,
Forest of Enchantment, or Le Mans, Forest of Majesty,
or even Gorre, Forest of the Dead, someone might have thought
to curry me, find me brackish water, perhaps comb
the chafing burrs from my hopelessly tangled mane.

But this was Morois, Forest of Love, and I just stumbled
forwards, and forwards again, as if there were no past
or future, waiting for that prick in my salty flank.

———

Everyone in This Story Speaks Except Me   *Iseult*

Even the words. The chords. The silence. I can only think.

I miss my father's Galway house, the crisp bed I made myself.
Call me ruthless but these days whirl forwards.
I am Queen of the Land of No Sleep. Why do they give me power?

I love him for no reason, as you might laugh at the pine breeze.
But he will test every gesture in Morois.

Once we could make each other strange as dawn just by undoing
one button, always the same button. Now we run to the shadows.

Once Satan appeared to Saint Marie d'Oignies and whispered,
This world is a dream. She answered, *Can't you hear the leper's bell?*

Now the first pines rise out of the cornrows, the elm crest
looms suddenly, we come to the threshold, the last hedgerow.

The horse rolls his red-veined eye. How Tristan must spur.
The Absolute drives him. The charm of wholeness.
But God is a broken man. A person and the loss of a person.

Yew branches draw back like bows. An opening will find us.
Now to learn what a servant knows. Cold and hunger.

How not to eat or sleep. How not to have a child.

Morois

The Play of Light and Shadow

Tristan

We want to give ourselves away utterly
but afterwards we resent it. It's the same
with the sparrows, their eyes burn so coldly
under the dusty pines, their small chests swell
as they dispute a crumb, or the empty place
where a seed was once. This is our law too,
to peck and peck at the self, to take turns
being *I*, to die in a fierce sidelong glance,
then to hold the entire thicket in one tilt
of a tufted head, to take flight suddenly
and fuck in midair, tumbling upwards.

Morois

Starving, we found one blackberry.
Since I picked it, I whispered, *you eat it.*
But I saw it first, she said, *so it's yours.*

I kissed her and pressed the globule with my tongue
into her mouth. Her tongue stopped me. She was shaking.

Was it sweet, I asked. *You swallowed it*, she said.

*

Morois: wilderness like any other except
the maple seeds whirl faster, eager to fall.

We were alone. What did I expect? Only the horse
stared lugubriously and turned his solemn rump.

Venus throbbed like a spider bite. Saturn towered over Gorre.

Already she had gathered thread-roots and floricane,
leery of the yellow stems that Satan pissed on.
Was she Majesty, or just an Irish farm girl?

The nightingale sang with his chest pressed
against a thorn, artfully wounded, practicing
to pour his heart out to no one.

The Fire

Kindle me with oak. I blaze grudgingly.
A log chars to ash
and falls apart at one touch.

Set me with laurel: blue-white glint,
comely as Jerusalem.

Thorn I light without a whiff of smoke.

Walnut I consume sweetly.
In sleep you'll feel the blessing
of requited love, not the terror.

Pulpy birch ignites in rain.

Yew is the tree of death and burns
slowly with unimaginable heat.

Rowan is holy and may not be culled.

Poplar flames easily but the smoke
will mask you like a caul
and make you feel desire has ended.

I am eager as a child, ardent like a suitor,
shy as a fugitive. At dawn
I grow brighter and a touch invisible
like the mind in old age.

I am faes. I have no self.
I come from the old religion
in which there are no martyrs.

———

*

Berthold of Regensberg says the odds for damnation
are 100,000 to 1, but that's for the pure of heart.
You are an adulterer, traitor and killer.

*

When you thought she might like you, you tried to
earn her. Now she loves you, you have no recourse.
You stand in a fire. Who are you, to be so chosen?
You whose strategy was to be a leaf in the forest?

The Living Spring

In my breathing shadow
the lovers hear their voices
confused with mine,
promising a slate roof,
a gate, a child, respite
from the Absolute.
Let them sleep.

Doesn't God love them
because they are like him,
too broken to obey
the rules of death?

In my ambit
birdsong is slurred,
nightingale's loneliness,
famished thrush, sparrow
pining in the cold,
each charged
with rapt indifference.

Rest while I tremble.
Isn't God himself
stubborn as water?

Moss Court   *Tristan*

I

I didn't know how to be in love in a forest.
I thought it would come to me, like music, or swimming.
I thought there would be two people. There was no one.
I hunted all day and found nothing but signs.
Boar drool hardened to a paste on an elder leaf,
signet-impress of its twisted toes in marl;
wolf's fumet neatly stacked beside the trail,
she-wolf droppings in the center, urine-scented;
mote of antler-velvet shining in a shaft of twilight;
template of the hare's dewlap, that track
melding to a giant handprint in green pollen;
faint skittish line of a lynx's dragging tail;
circular wave in a pond that meant the bear
had been scaring fish to the banks; hoof mark
still glinting with black ventricle blood;
deer-girdled birch. But never a sighting.
Those woods were silent except for birds
crying danger, or sexual longing, or bragging
of their prowess, or praising the slanted light.

I climbed a towering cedar. The coarse bark
tore my hands, but sweet-smelling gum cauterized me.
Ladder-branches began to give, the tip buckled,
but all I saw was Morois, oak and pine,
each crest shining with a different light, so many
the eye could not linger on one. That canopy
trembled as a lover might shake with desire
mixed with a little distaste.
                               Far away

I saw Brocéliande, Forest of Enchantment, same sheen
of pollen, identical sway, perhaps a few more sycamore.
Beyond that, Gorre, Forest of the Dead, identical,
similar play of light and shadow, maybe a preponderance
of pale-flowered yew. Then Le Mans, Forest of Majesty,
too distant to distinguish. At last a faint smudge
as if scratched with charcoal, that might be the ocean.
I clambered down. My horse looked at me pityingly:
Now you know where you are?   It was night. I'd killed nothing.

2

Iseult baked bread from acorns and spikelets of false oat.
She stewed fungi that protrude like visors from the pines.
She dug wild barley, sorghum, darnel and melick,
dandelion shoots and burdock root. Her hands
grew hard, nails caked with granitic dust.

3

My Queen followed a black Monarch to sarnica,
stalking jaggedly, so it would not hide and fold its wings.
She unearthed argenta where the stones are dappled and sweaty.
She dug up self-heal at the springhead, there where the woods
feel emptiest. From comfrey she distilled an elixir
that soothed the throbbing of my wound. She made a mint poultice
that calmed my fear of death, and a balm of verbena
so I no longer feared my own strength, or hers, or the enemy's.

She found black currants, and tart green gooseberries
striated with stretch-marks, a feast, but ruinous.
My love's skin grew slack, her eyes enormous,
and she was my only mirror—in the snowmelt pools
desire erased my face and etched in a fool's beseeching gape.

4
We explored each other and found our own spring,
taproot, firestone and deep shade.

We held our own court. Without rules of precedence
we flinched at a withheld glance.

We played chess naked, knight against queen.
The bishop was a slanting hornet, the rook a toadstool,
God the pawn who alone can change. The king
was a spindled leaf.

5
I followed the trail of a woodpecker whose claws
pointed backwards, whose self-satisfied hammering
maddened me, when I heard a crash in the thornbushes
and notched my bow.

          That force that keeps us from acting
in dreams—God?—stayed my hand and my dog came gasping
through razor vines, so skinny his ribs hurt to touch.
He fell at my feet and licked my ankle feebly.

I carried him home. Iseult started: *Game?* Then sobbed.

How did he find us, so deep in the wild?

He drank the philtre too, she said.

Her Mirror

TRISTAN AND ISEULT GO TOGETHER

She	I
made	am
a	growing
looking glass	old
of	in
a	a
mica	vast
shard	forest
and	with
stared	a
into	lover
it	who
though	can't
all	catch
she	rabbits
could	and
see	a
was	dog
the	with
flicker	colic—
of	even
an	the
eyelash,	horse
a	is
mole,	skinny
or	and
the	longs
dark	to
glitter	be
of	shod
evening	and
itself	primped.
.	.

LIKE GRIEF AND LONELINESS

——————

43

Ceol Sidhe

Tristan

She cut herself a harp from green rowan
that only the faes may cull.

She stood in the scrim of ash leaves
wielding my sword without permission.

I thought we would negotiate
in the wild, she would be less a Queen.
But no. Each day she wears her robe and crown
more imperiously, though they are pollen and dew.

Who am I, not even an audience, a gawker,
bystander at the heart of my own Adventure?

The strings she spindled from mulberry root,
guts of a snared vole, and the Master,
Re, from her cloth-of-gold sleeve.

The pegs were willow, the waist and belly ash.

Without being asked, she scoured my sword
with horsetail ferns and creek-bottom sand,
and left that Damascene blade sharper.

All dusk I watched her tune, testing each note
against a pitch that does not exist.
Then she began the labor of undoing, tempering
each Absolute before it imposed a system.

At last the strings moved like living rain.
Was she listening in those austere chords
for a command, a secret message? From whom?

———

44

She held her wrist cocked, motionless, while her thumbs
inscribed circles, like a wasp groping for a scent,
after the style of the Morne Mountain masters.

Her silence deepened, clarified, and became harmony.

She played heedlessly, flawlessly, like a woman waking
after long sleep, or settling to meat after famine.

She sang thinly, in a language I can't understand,
Alaric, Mogrian, or High Welsh. Once I heard my name
and thrilled to its strangeness on those half-parted lips.
But she turned away from me, away from the fire,
towards the glade where the eye of an animal
or basilisk or lost soul gleamed like a pinhole.

Then I heard Mark, the name Logres, and her voice
modulated in dirge rhythm to the extreme past
as if that were a thirteenth key. All night I watched
as the shadows the flame cast, flame-colored themselves,
bowed to her, because she was Queen, or because she was keening.

Surely if she loved me, the key would be ecstasy—
to be alone together, secluded in a forest?

She was like God, she didn't want intimacy,
just to be right, always right, like the wind and rain.

Once or twice she lost her place and counted a few bars
in my language, but backwards, to the correct measure.

At dawn she cleared her throat and wrapped the harp
in a cinquefoil wimple I'd given her and huddled
naked under jute in straw. I knelt beside her
until my knees ached, listening to her breath
in case I might interpret a catch.

———————

She smelled of deer tallow with which she greased
her shanks against the cold, and crushed basil.

I thought I heard the exile harp answer her
from the direction of Brocéliande, modulating carefully,
like a spider descending a thread, minor to diminished.

At last the sun rose, light tightened like a bass string
in withered alder branches, then slackened. It was day.
The finches sang freely, in pairs, each to each,
and there too I heard my name, forwards and backwards,
and hers, the King's, and the hour of our death.

The Self

When
we
rolled
in mottled
oak leaves
I
shone,
though
the high
hawk
saw
just
two
naked
fugitives.

The Mandrake Root   *Tristan*

I hunted at night under unbroken canopy.
I spread out my palms to sense the gaps
and wriggled through like a man being born.
I memorized my steps, to find the way back,
though they existed only in my mind
where nothing can be undone. Sometimes
I sensed the cry of something suffering
breathlessly, and let an arrow fly but heard
just the twang, whoosh, and feather-draft,
faint creak of my sinews contracting.

I imagined I was in bed with Iseult
and struggled to open my eyes, but no resistance,
so they must be open. I reminded myself
if I were asleep I would be able to dream *dawn*—
helpless not to dream it, for the name contains it.

Here there was just darkness as if I had entered
stale air inside a skull, then a faint gleam.
I knew it was the mandrake, that shines all night.
I couldn't believe my happiness.

I dug with my nails and yanked from the clay
a little root gleaming coldly, knowingly,
shaped like a tiny man—perfect eyes,
closed; wrinkled nose; tiny fingers—
I counted them: ten; sex like a bud.

I cradled that lump and found my way home
and cried, *Love, love.* Iseult came running
with a torn panse, thinking I was wounded.

I handed her the manikin and explained
our sorrow had ended, from the juice
she could brew a liquor that would ease our loneliness.

But she just stared, white-lipped, then took it
and hugged it a little savagely—it shone
a tad brighter for her and suddenly faded

to dull loam—dawn had broken, the sky was bloody,
the forest full of cries. *Suffering*, I explained,
these plants can suffer, but she held
a finger to my lips and whispered *Shush*.
I heard the shouts of huntsmen.

Morte

The horns sounded Relaye: two long motes and one strake.
I heard the yawp of the dogs taking on every emotion,
every sound in every language, feeling too much to speak,
feeling too much to feel. The trumpet sounded Prise,
four long motes (the last once cracked) and at that
every horn in the forest—who knew there were so many?—
responded. But I Tristan, Master of the Hunt,
perched like a finch in the vase-crest of the high elm,
I watched the Unmaking and had to bite my tongue
when a veneur used a ladle and not tongs
to tease out the liver. Directly under me
the tenentmen carried the hart from the forest.
First the great twelve-pointed antlered head
with its unswerving open eye. Then, one on each side,
the proud shoulders. Then the spine, the haunches,
the scrotum nailed to a peeled willow stick,
the chine and hindquarters, each on one flank.
The drum pounded softly. The heart
had been given to the dogs who feasted numbly,
gravely, exhausted by the magnitude beyond foreknowledge
of their labor, their attainment, and their reward.
I knew all their names—Psyche, Chloe, Phytis—
but nothing would have made them look up.
When they were gone, and the children
who had killed a deer made of whorled birch bark
had finished bickering over the spoils,
I shinnied down and licked the snow—
thick black blood from the central ventricle.
I held a little in my mouth to share with my Queen.
I began loping back along the berms of the clearings,
trailing a cedar branch to cover my tracks,

bounding sideways, doubling back to accent my scent
so it would seem to fade when I crept north,
slithering down the veins of a frozen stream.
I found my Queen hunched in her samite rags.
She tensed in my arms. I felt or tried to feel
a little blush in her cheeks and I begged her,
Lie with me: and she: No: and I begged:
and she: not even No: just silence.
Then she huddled beside me, more silence than woman,
the wind proceeded in the high bare branches,
and it was as before, when we were still wooing,
before we loved each other more than God.

Her Decision   *Tristan*

1
Her mind is like the elm, shag-barked and vase-cresting.
Her consent is like mossy ground, secreting dangerous give.

Her will is a swiftly advancing radiant cloud,
always the same but different, trailing deep shadow.

2
Once knights hammered each other to pig-iron
for one crook of her little finger.

Now Iseult shivers beside me, her bitter resolve
hops like a sparrow in frost-tinged sedge.

Her decisions are irrevocable. She doesn't know she made them.
I must make her confess she found my flaw. She'll leave me.

Easier to convince nightfall and the violent elm leaves
whirling on a fixed point that exists nowhere.

3
When I lie on top, or under her, my mind clears
and I can analyze our situation: winter coming,

acorn bread, twig bed, even the dog growing sullen.
All other times, my brain swarms with Absolutes.

4
We troubadour-knights are the first to practice *fin'amor*.
Our fathers were brutes, our grandfathers dripping spears.

I believe in the donnai, the assag, but within reason.
Let her control me, but just for a harp cadence.

But we are stranded in eternity, in Morois. Here God
moves in the pines like a breeze that knows what it is.

The Other World

3

With every second thought, Tristan builds
the other world, out of moth quiver,
dangling webs, shudder-path of a dragonfly
suspended a blink in shafts of evening—
from cumulus shadow and impending rain
his axe-mind hacks Yes and No—
he can't stand her reproof, can't bear her smile.
He adores her but shouldn't, she doesn't love him
but must, summer but winter, red-eyed monster
or pure knight, he is Tantris, his wound throbs—

2

that other world is Ysinvitrain,
Glass Island, where the eye can see itself,
a lover's will is transparent, that twig bed
is softer than this, those great oaks
soak up calcium and sap, these pines
wither: there love is action,
here it is a sigh.

I

Tomorrow the King will find the fugitives
as they doze exhausted in a piney neck
and spare them, leaving his sword
to shine between their bodies.
Fortune will reverse.

The King's Sword

King Mark
discovered us
among spindled
elm leaves and put
his naked sword
between us softly
not to wake us.
He ruined me—
how could my love
be equal to his?
He had *fin' amor*,
mine was *fol*.
I hid the weapon
and resolved then
to win her back
by slaying giants—
Toriax, Beliagog—,
and monsters;
the flesh-eating
mare Xanthus,
the Monoceros,
part-horse,
part-elephant,
woman's gaze;
next I would find
the Sangrail
and bring her that
glory as a gift:
where if not
in Morois,
Forest of Love?

I
am
Hellebore
forged
in
hot
beds,
now
laid
between
naked
lovers
in
cold
dew
to
rust
as
they
tremble.
My
blade
severs.
Once
I
killed,
now
I
spare
without
mercy.

I dreamt my husband
forgave us and asked
that we return to
Logres, I his wife,
Tristan his son,
there to grow old
in peace without
this long loneliness
God knew when all
he had to talk to
was Logos. I thought
I bathed and toweled
my newborn child.
Brangien pardoned
me and brought
us salt and plain
wine with no charm
except drunkenness.
She combed my hair
and the ash harp
was unstrung and
could not sing
my betrayal. I woke
in tears and turned
to tell Tristan
but beside me
just the template
of his prone body
and a snake-track
that shone faintly
in red dust.

The Dog

The horse Beau Joueur, who should be called Gros Joueur,
keeps me awake all night rubbing his rump against smooth beech.
He snorts, deliberately loud. He has nothing to do
except chomp delicious melick: talk about a forest of love!

I followed my masters here because they are helpless
like God or a poor man in the wind and rain.
I tore my coat. Who notices? Who pets me?
They sniff each other like poodles, but with more drama.

If they scold, it is each other, if they wander off
it is from each other, if they train anyone to fetch,
sit, roll over, it is the Other, the undying love.
What hell it must be to hunt on such a tangled leash.

Me they praise absently. *Good Dog!* The Other
has a thousand faults which they tally in secret
until a tirade overflows: *You Always . . . you Never . . .*

Inwardly they denounce each other, but to whom?
The trees can't understand them. Neither can the music,
too high-pitched for their hearing. The birds don't care.

Because they are lovers, each second they share
is eternity, fate drives them forwards,
they have no clue how to scamper, how to prance.

Sex baffles them. Victory or defeat? Why always more so?
Fucking makes their bodies a thorny thicket.
She flinches at his wound. He cries for her loneliness.

Perhaps through the scrim of desire they may glimpse
the actual forest: alder leaves like wringing hands,
a nuthatch marching straight up a tall cedar.

These woods are full of deer, boar, elk and bear,
but the lovers' longing is a magic cloak
that makes all other creatures invisible.

I have to guard them from wind, rain, and their minds.
They fascinate me, like the small dead things in the sedge.

Tristan losing footing, manacled by his arguments.
Iseult who misses salt, bells, and his absence.

All night they moan, or choose not to, the horse farts,
and I have no Other except a touch of gray along my muzzle
I can glimpse by squinting: maybe I too am dying of love?

Hunting over the Border in Brocéliande   *Tristan*

Before dawn, I saw my first monster.
A little wyvern, crouching behind a birch—
as if a birch could hide a wyvern!—
with a wrinkled nose and flaring nostrils
and muddy eyes, in which I saw death.
I knew: when it pretends to flee,
that's the moment of danger, the spade tail
is razor sharp. I mimed terror.
I notched an arrow. I didn't even aim,
just thought *wyvern*. I sighted
the notch in the *y*, the chink
in those reptile scales. I killed it
within the allotted minute. I tried
to drag the body home. My wound throbbed.
The hide grew cold and gave off fumes.
I left it strewn with beech leaves
like a vine-covered stump.

I told the Queen and she sighed
and made love to me, but her eyes
were on the high swift clouds.

At the onset of winter
I tracked a basilisk
by its smoldering footprints.
The elms were scorched, their leaves singed.
I had come to Gorre, borderland
that has no marker and no guard.
I polished my shield with creek sand
for only the terror of the snake's eyes can kill it.
That reptile body shuddered and turned to stone.

———

The firedrake wandered from the north
at the first frost, when Iseult nagged for a roof.
I fenced against its flames
with the wind of my vaulting body—
tierce, prime, balestra—and slaughtered it.

The amphisbaena, heads on both ends of its snake body,
one snout drooling, the other grinning,
glimpsed me, placed one head in the other mouth,
and rolled towards me, one eye after the other
fixing me with a dazzling episodic stare.

As the last leaves fell, I met the miraj,
the horned rabbit, whose sideways kick
is lethal, who confuses you with the shame
defeat would bring (and once or twice
I did back away), and the traitor dog
who pretends to fetch a stick
but only wants to eat your heart.

So that was why there was no game
in those trackless woods—no wardens,
no pursuers: the rule of monsters . . .

Iseult still made room for me in the ferns,
perhaps she sighed, but I felt the inch
between us watch me like an eye.

One twilight I met Nebuchadnezzar.
Maddened by age, he had grown talons.
I asked if he knew where mushrooms grow,
or succulent roots, but he just grinned,
shitting himself in the moss.

The manticore, with a human face and lion body,
that shoots darts from its anus,
summoned me with an absurd faint high voice

---

like a cracked tin trumpet.
Tantris, it called, as if I were my opposite.

My heart stopped when I heard the phoenix
singing itself on fire in its high nest
lined with nard and coriander.
The power of that music is superhuman.
I memorized a few notes for Iseult.

Once the shadow of a roc passed, too high to kill.

When the sedge shone with rime, the Questing Beast
slunk towards Le Mans, baying,
part deer, part hound, and I knew
the Grail must be close, deeply hidden.

As the ground froze, I found many creatures
that were part of other creatures:
the panotii, whose huge ears are wings-—
I argued them out of the sky
when they tried to flap away;
the monoceros, horse body, elephant feet,
stag's tail; the onocentaur
with his beautiful eyes and huge sex;
the blennies, golden locusts
with the faces of women. I looked
for Iseult's gray stare, and spared that one.

Sometimes Houdain, lost in his bone-bitch trance,
walked straight through an ichneumon or blemmya.

When I thought I'd cleansed those woods of monsters
I met the cantoplas, so ravenous
it gnaws its own shins. That creature terrified me.
I notched my arrow trembling.

I told the Queen I had seen the Grail,
a gold chalice that moves of its own will
in a straight line, like a winter firefly.
I was allowed to touch it. It burned me
with a cold fire because I was pure,
then disappeared among the pines.

But she sighed and turned to the wall.

Always silent, that dark Queen!

A first snowflake glistened in her unbound hair.

When I woke, she had returned to Logres.

Avalon

Folie Tristan

1
No more monsters. Just gray trees.

I lost my mind and Iseult.

I squeeze my way between thoughts.

I have stumbled out of the Adventure.

No is the exit. She reigns in her Kingdom.

2
I bite my finger to remember the loneliness

I felt when I lay beside her.

3
God loves freedom so bitterly

he abandoned me, so I might taste it.

4
No dawn. Withered leaves. I forget their names.

This life has no name: why should a tree?

But the next world: Avalon, Ysinvitrain,

the Fortunate Island, the Land of the Living . . .

5
Only numbers, driving forwards.

Gray trees. So tall there is no horizon.

Black Winter Stars   *Tristan*

It's death you love, not her, said the rock dove,
fixing me with a bright muddy eye. A vein in its neck pulsed.

How could a bird be so wrong? *If I loved death, would I burn,*
here where nothing lasts? You just peck to peck, I said,
where there is no worm, no crumb: therefore your name.

*

You confused Iseult with your mother, said a sparrow archly,
hopping in the space between words. *I have no mother,* I said.
She pulled me with her own fine hands from her belly and died
there, in Logres, in the withered birch forest.

Even the gravel-voiced grackles fell silent, embarrassed.
Perhaps I shouldn't have added, *but the Queen named me Tantris.*

*

The starlings spoke in High Welsh. When I couldn't follow
they rose and performed pentagrams and spirals in the night sky.
I understood: a blueprint for the Castle You Come to Unawares.

*

The grosbeak, who discards the plum and eats the stone,
is preparing to go. But the wren will stay with me.
It loves pinecones and the way you can see a certain distance in ice.

*

The leaves lose their hold, and each talks to itself in midair.
The beech leaf discovers why it has that sawtooth edge
—to grip the breeze—and the oak why it has deep bays:
to whoosh, to tumble, to land softly, to scritch a few inches.

*

Even the stones speak to me, complaining how I separate them,
lover from loved one, with the toe of my felt boot.

I am my stubborn opposite. The robin left long ago
when the first snow wrote in the massive pines

her mind is transparent and her will impenetrable.

An Opening

I searched for the hollow where we once lay.
It seemed the timothy tips were still bent,
the sedge sticky, the ants jittery.

I came to a circle of split stones.
I knew it for the old fire and collected peat moss,
antler velvet and birch bark, and struck flint
but the flame that rose gave no heat.
I could put my hand in it and watch the nail blacken
and begin to curl inwards, and still feel nothing.
And I had thought madness was suffering.
Time did not pass. The coals flinched, the sparks
launched themselves like soundless bees.
There was no connection between char and ash.
Dawn was a paler, more begrudging midnight.
I couldn't tell the sun from the hole it made in heaven.
I couldn't feel God's grace though it burned a hole in me.

Sometimes in my madness I tried to love myself
but my hand grew tired, and felt betrayed.
My sex was like her: adamant, too smooth.

I tried to strike myself with my sword
just to have a grievance to occupy my empty mind.
I heard it whistle towards me and resigned myself
to hell, since this was mortal sin. But no.
The blade sundered my stunned shadow.
I stood apart, watching, profoundly watching,
as if the world had become a picture of itself.

I dreamed Iseult would love me, and she did.
I had to test it, as if it happened in sleep.

Like any servant, wind and rain broke me.
I dreamed I would go mad, and I am.

I dreamed I would become you, the listener,
and find a clearing in the forest.

The Grail

I am a smashed robin's egg,
a hollow acorn the beetle drilled,
a cup with a hairline crack
that holds the world to come.

The Grail

Morois Morois Morois Morois Morois Morois Morois Morois Morois Morois
Morois Morois Morois Morois Morois Morois Morois Morois Morois Morois
Morois Morois Morois Morois Morois Morois Morois Morois Morois Morois
Morois Morois Morois Morois Morois Morois Morois Morois Morois Morois
Morois Morois Morois Morois Morois Morois Morois Morois Morois Morois
Morois Morois Morois Morois Morois Morois Morois Morois Morois Morois
Morois Morois Morois Morois Morois Morois Morois Morois Morois Morois
Morois Morois Morois Morois Morois Morois Morois Morois Morois Morois
Morois Morois Morois Morois Morois Morois Morois Morois Morois Morois
Morois Morois Morois Morois Morois Morois Morois Morois Morois Morois
Morois Morois Morois Morois Morois Morois Morois Morois Morois Morois
Morois Morois Morois Morois Morois Morois Morois Morois Morois Morois
Morois Morois   Morois Morois
Morois Morois   Morois Morois
Morois Morois Morois   Morois Morois Morois
Morois Morois Morois Morois   Morois Morois Morois Morois
Morois Morois Morois Morois Morois Morois Morois Morois Morois Morois
Morois Morois Morois Morois Morois Morois Morois Morois Morois Morois
Morois Morois Morois Morois Morois Morois Morois Morois Morois Morois
Morois Morois Morois Morois Morois Morois Morois Morois Morois Morois
Morois Morois Morois Morois Morois Morois Morois Morois Morois Morois
Morois Morois Morois Morois Morois Morois Morois Morois Morois Morois
Morois Morois Morois Morois Morois Morois Morois Morois Morois Morois
Morois Morois Morois Morois Morois Morois Morois Morois Morois Morois
Morois Morois Morois Morois Morois Morois Morois Morois Morois Morois
Morois Morois Morois Morois Morois Morois Morois Morois Morois Morois

The Adventure of Tristan and Iseult

I am growing old. I am starting to fade.
I am increasingly tongue-tied.
With great pains and blandishments
the harpist coaxes me to the Re string.

There I last only a few measures—
spasm on silk sheets, come in a forest,
mad eye of a dying monster, sizzling
like yolk on a griddle.   Then diminuendo.

The text is filling with lacunae:
[. . .] ash leaf with an erratic vein [. . .]
[. . .] red nubbin on a spruce twig [. . .]
[. . .] basswood in a halo of bees [. . .]

The chronicler pauses, his mind full of twilight.
He chooses fresh pumice and abrades the vellum—
caul of a stillborn calf—and starts to doodle
in the soft margin.
                        Tristan will stop muttering
and learn to live in hours instead of eternity.
Iseult will apologize, form alliances, rule.

They tell lies. They come to know themselves
despite the philtre, the pines, and the King's fury,
out of habit and grievance. They too fade.

That love endures, cold as the wind and rain.

Armorica

Another Iseult, who didn't know my faults, might be easier—
a demure girl I didn't love so much, and there were many
in that foggy neatly tilled country I escaped to: Iseult
of the White Hands, Iseult of the Red Lips, Iseult
of the Flaxen Hair. I married the first who said yes,
though in bed I felt just the throbbing of my wound.

Other Tristans crowded the taverns—perhaps the harp
had made our names common as our destiny:
Tristan the Better Lover, Tristan the Less Mad.
I tried to avoid them: one less petulant quarrel
over who killed a vole or rabbit. I made a living
hunting small monsters, no bigger than a crayfish
or prawn, and giving private fencing lessons.

Time closed like a book. My wound stung less,
a diminishing music. I who once pretended
to be mad, and went mad, now disguised myself
with white whiskers. I became reasonable, remote:
Maybe things will work out, maybe the world will end,
I thought. I enjoyed the local cuisine: bisque,
ratatouille, and a chalk-white plummy Vouvray.
I savored a village renown, and the jealousy
of ancient cankered harpers. My body began to fail.

Sickness marked me with its waxy pencil
and called me in its coy voice, by my opposite name:
"Come here, Tantris." At once my days shortened
towards that winter whose wind I shall not feel.
The tip of the yew leaf curled inwards.

———

Then I had a caravel fitted out, with ash oars,
a damask bed, and red sails so I would not live
in case of *No*.

I sent it to Logres with my last silver coin,
certain she would come, certain it would be too late.

Red Sail

I am the deliberate misunderstanding between two lovers. I unify them more surely than joy. Why do they need my fixed sign? Dye me in cochineal, fold me along careful seams, stow me under brass locks. When the crew hoists me, how quickly the caravel luffs, yaws, and cuts a dividing wake towards Armorica, kingdom of long parallel furrows.

Queen of the Land of No Sleep

Iseult

1

I didn't hesitate. I adore him. But what were my choices?
Deny the Adventure or die of plague with a Tristan
fussed over by a mild wife with mushroom-white hands?
I hear him argue: *everyone who dies dies of love*.
Suffering gives him that right?

So be it, little mad knight whose madness cooled
in a colder bed. No more ziphius, no more ichneumon.
Iseult is still your monster.

Every great love has an obstacle. Ours was us.
The Law was carved in us like a child's name in a tree.

2

The Chronicle tells the rest fairly accurately.
I packed nothing and rode to the port at dawn
with many a backwards glance at Brangien,
who didn't wave, knowing I would never return.
I found Tristan's ship behind a stand of willows
whose roots must have been immune to salt,
growing right down to the ocean. I remanded the horse
in excellent custody. I hailed the captain
who scooped up his dice lazily and greeted me
with a shrug. Tristan's charm was wearing off the world.

The end you know. How the storm battered us.
The purser wanted to throw me overboard for Syax
but the cabin boy argued I was faes. I was used to that.

Then the calm came. That sea was not just transparent
but seemed to magnify my gaze. Pearls glinted
on the close seafloor. The water shone thinner
than in a human ocean. The oar had no purchase
and flailed through that radiance.

The delay-fish had latched on to our rudder
and no oar or punting pole could dislodge it.

How the crew missed their wives and lovers!
To catch the faintest breath of twilight
they piled on sail after sail. They hoisted
Tristan's satin bedsheets, then the red sail
whose import will kill him,

and I did not command them not to
and cannot say why not.

The Land of the Living   *Tristan*

I closed my eyes and felt the light break.
I was whole at last but the world around me
divided and through that dark water
a ship came to take me to Avalon.

Three Queens huddled at the prow:
Morgana le Fay, the Queen of North Gales,
the Queen of the Empty Kingdom.

I asked them by signs, since it is not permitted
to the newly dead to speak—where was Iseult?

They answered: she was waiting for me on the island,
or so I understood their gestures: a woman combing air.

The breeze freshened and that small sloop yawed
up the veined flanks of breakers and lolled in the troughs.

The yard swung of its own accord, tacked,
at once I smelled peat fire and bread baking.

A dog yapped in greeting. For whom? We had no more scent.

While I was still I I heard
a siskin calling in the fog,

grate of the keel, a rasping broom,
clank of a leper's bell.

The King's Prison

Coda

I

They burned my harp. They said it was faes.
They cut the strings and called me
a chronicler of heretic adulterers.

They dressed me like a doll
in the sanbenito, a burlap sack
meticulously adorned with the image
of the fire, if that can be rendered
in madder-dyed thread, and the corazo,
huge dunce cap that made me stoop
at the threshold of the narrow door.

I learned these terms when children pointed.

Also I wore the yellow cross, emblem
of my crime, which I confess freely—
I saw God's will in the bolt drawn shut.

*

Such a tall wheel, on oiled hinges,
so many accessories, each a matching lampblack:
rope, hook, brake: such a flourish
to wheel it out (how else),
then the introductory questions:

Do I believe God pardons lovers?
Is that mercy conditional or absolute,
immediate or slow, lightning or steady rain?

83

I swear they recorded their questions
in a fat gilt-bound book
but when I answered as best I could
confined to yes and no, their minds wandered,
the skittering nib fell silent.
I trailed off. There was a sudden deep hush.
They shook themselves (dogs emerging from a lake)
and prepared me as if I were a bride
being plucked and hennaed.

They broke me: what else could the wheel do?
and recorded it
as if there could have been an alternative.

A cricket sang in that vault.

I prayed to the neutral angels
who don't side with God or Satan
and a thrush called faintly, unused to being heard
by someone who was not I.

Then the silence was profound.
You could hear the scritch of the nib
copying the questions
from scroll to scroll.

They showed me the calcinated willow pegs.

2
They stretched me. I exaggerated a little—
I said I had committed obscene crimes:
glorified lust, denied divine right,
that I was free, I loved God intolerably,
so that the gears and straps felt like nothing
compared to the suffering of that fire
and by patience, labor, and prayer (they prayed too),
they added an inch to me on the rack.

They crossed my name from the book of life
but added a few extra letters
and inked in a few cursives
so that I will never be deciphered.

Now my name is breath
and the nephilim comfort me.
They wash and bind my wounds.

3
Such a rage to pose questions.
Why does God permit sin?
Why does he pardon traitors?

Why did he allow his own son to die?
Why can't he return to the past
and deflect the lance from that naked flank—
why must he move forwards, always forwards?
What drives him?

Under the thumbscrew
my responses were random, perhaps just grunts—
maybe they trusted them
because they were given by suffering, not a person,
as if a broken jug could talk, or a useless inch of string—
they nodded to themselves.

Clearly they had lived a long time
with just questions and answers
and the slow mounting cry
was a better possibility. They inscribed it
in a fat book—no doubt all vowels—
which made it part of history:

a complicated game between good and evil,
memorized by children, carved in the plinth
of marble statues, not something that actually happens

---

to a thumb, a tiny part of the body,
less than a thousandth of its weight,

nothing that could dare to call itself I
or be commemorated, though it breaks
like a man, a kingdom, a belief.

Acknowledgments

A section of "The Grail" (in the chapter entitled "Logres") appeared in *The Paris Review* under the title "Morois."

A version of "Coda" also appeared in *The Paris Review*.

A different section of "The Grail" (in the chapter entitled "Logres") is excerpted from "Mission to Gorre," which appeared in the *St. Petersburg Review*.

"The Play of Light and Shadow" appeared in *Poetry*.

Thanks to the John Simon Guggenheim Foundation and the American Academy of Arts and Letters, for support that helped me write this book.

Thanks to the MacDowell Colony, the Virginia Center for the Creative Arts, and the Corporation of Yaddo, for their kindness.

Sources consulted for *Love in the Last Days* include *The Romance of Tristan and Iseult* (compiled by Joseph Bédier), *Tristan: With the Surviving Fragment of the "Tristan of Thomas"* (compiled by Gottfried von Strassburg), *The Béroul Mannuscript, The Hawk and the Hound: The Art of Medieval Hunting* by John Cummins, *The Irish Harp* by Joan Rimmer, "The Battle of the Trees" essay by Robert Graves in his *The White Goddess*, "Lévi-Strauss in Broceliande: A Brief Analysis of a Courtly Romance" essay by Jacques Le Goff in his *The Medieval Imagination, Of Giants: Sex, Monsters, and the Middle Ages* by Jeffrey Jerome Cohen, *L'Erotique des Troubadours* by René Nelli, *Tristan et Yseut* (Bibliothèque de la

Pléiade), *Feudal Society* by Marc Bloch, and *Le Morte d'Arthur* by Thomas Malory.

Thanks to the staff of the General Research Division, Rose Reading Room, New York Public Library, for their invaluable assistance.

Special thanks to my editor, Deborah Garrison, to Marc Kaminsky, and to Richard Hoffman.

This book is dedicated to the memory of Marc Bloch.

A Note About the Author

D. Nurkse is the author of ten previous books of poetry. His recent prizes include a Literature Award from the American Academy of Arts and Letters and a Guggenheim fellowship. He has also written on human rights.

A Note on the Type

This book was set in Fairfield, a typeface designed by the American artist and engraver Rudolph Ruzicka (1883–1978).

Composed by North Market Street Graphics,
Lancaster, Pennsylvania

Printed and bound by Thomson-Shore,
Dexter, Michigan

Design by Michael Collica